Winding Ways

FRAN ORENSTEIN

Aquitaine, Ltd.
Phoenix, Arizona

Cover design by JD Smith Designs

ISBN-10: 0-9914843-4-7
ISBN-13: 978-09914843-4-8

www.aquitaineltd.com

DEDICATION

For
Adele Siegel
Georgine Brave
Stefanie Mandelbaum
Judith Chinery
Barbara Pointon

My forever friends who have shared the sorrows and the joys,
and walked the path.

CONTENTS

THE MIDDLE YEARS

And so we move inexorably on through yet
another passage, where the turns are less sharp,
the crossroads less defined and the road less
serpentine; a passage of reflection and choices.

PRELUDE

Winding Ways brings us into the second part of this exiting journey called life. Seasons change, the sun rises and sets, the planet turns, and time moves on to the gentle ticking of the clock. Bodies shrink and wrinkles awaken unbidden to match greying hair and aching bones as we grow older with each passing year.

With our first breath we prepare for the last sigh. It is what happens in between that sets us apart establishing our legacy. Follow the many paths we trod from early middle years to early elder years, but beware trolls that lie in wait under the bridges, dragons that lurk in their caves and sharks that patrol the waters. Life is not an easy passage, for it may be riddled with pitfalls. Life can also be filled with joyful abundance and love. The choice is ours, and the best will happen if we follow our dream and live it as though it were a fabulous journey from beginning to end.

Walk with me as we rejoice in a rainbow, the trill of a finch, the scent of freshly mowed grass, white cloud puffs turning orange and red at sunset, the shadow of the sun on the mountains at dusk, and sparkling water reflecting a blue sky. Let us leave our footprints in the sand until the tide laps them up. Please make sure you laugh along the way.

DR. FRAN ORENSTEIN, AUGUST 5, 2015

A QUEST

She calls herself The Wanderer
Roaming the country on a quest
Seeking the elusive answer,
Flowing just beyond her reach

She writes upon the sands of time
Only to find her words
Swept away by circumstance
Stabbed by ignorance

She reaches out to heal
Pushed away by disbelievers
Laughing behind cupped hands
She shakes her head and moves on

Ever wandering, seeking solace
In shallow acquaintances
Not understanding the meaningless
Words and gestures of false friends

Trusting at first, then suspicion
Followed by doubt, cemented by betrayal
The shame of failure haunting her
Hiding in a cave within her mind

THE PRISTINE PATH

Step upon the pristine path
A lane not traveled
Untrammeled by life's detritus
Awaiting one soul

Brave enough to follow the road
On an uncharted journey
A new life
Unique unto herself

Twists and turns may lead to futures
Yet unknown
Mysterious adventures
Byways to explore

Thrilling anticipation of new realms
Of possibilities unknown
Awaiting one intrepid
Set of footprints in the dirt

THE FACES OF FRIENDSHIP

First friend, a mother's face
smiling from a lofty perch
seemingly adrift from bodily form
floating in and out of sight.

Friendly hands reaching out
to comfort, to cuddle and soothe.
Hands that hold the milk of life
sating the primal need.

Many faces, gentle, scary, funny
strange and unrecognizable
in the cacophony of coos,
overwhelming the tiny psyche.

Children, floating in and out
like clouds wandering across the sky,
connecting, dissipating, reconnecting,
linked in wispy trails of tenuous bonds.

Some attach for a lifetime.
Others drift into memories
of forgotten names and faces
hovering at the perimeter of the mind.

A hint here and there of shared times,
games played, won and lost,
discovery, sacred handshakes,
secrets whispered behind cupped hands.

Adolescent angst arguing with anxiety

amid intolerable images of self.
First love and first realization of reality,
as imploding values explode friendships
Surviving friendships endure forever,
at least as long as each shall live,
across continents and oceans,
bolstered by shared remembrances.

Adult friendships forged by mutual interest,
nurtured by the need to belong.
Firmly rooted in mature foundations
of understanding and acceptance

Lasting friendships entrenched
by jointly forged memories
embracing life experiences
beyond mundane daily humdrum.

Aged friendships created by expediency.
The desperate need for human connection
to ward off the encroaching loneliness
of approaching finality.

Friendships without foundation
without a prologue,
ethereal, expedient and never-lasting
beyond the moment of connection.

Clouds dissipating quickly,
pulling apart, reaching for the next one,
separating and drifting,
blowing into the firmament
From first wail to last exhale
forever friends, enduring to the end,

Fran Orenstein

or acquaintances journeying together,
all entwined for a brief flicker in time.

ENDINGS

It's a fatal disease.
And the day fell apart
Too many people
Leaving forever

She wrote a poem
I wept in anger, frustration
Despair tore my heart
I sent her a poem back

I WONDER~HER WORDS

I wonder if you'll think of me
      When I've gone away
I wonder if you'll think of
      All the silly things I'd say

I wonder if you'll remember
      How I look
I wonder if you'll sit under
      The big tree
With my name carved in stone
      The gentle tears will flow

Then I wonder will you come at all?

TEARS~POET'S RESPONSE

Your poem wrenched my heart
Tears overflowed my eyes
My chest burned with silent sobs
        Of anguished pain

As long as I breathe life
You will live forever
And I'll recall the feisty one
        Who took on causes

The strong and beautiful you
Taking up the fight
Other's abandoned in a quest
        To save a tree

The smart and sassy gal
Who cared about her kids
Her grandkids and her once love
        Always there for them

So perhaps in body I can't come
But in memory, I'm there
I'll remember you,
        A friendship cherished

And one day we will meet again
In poetry and laughter
Now tears obscure the words
        And I don't want to say goodbye

So the ending...fight on

Do whatever it takes
To keep life going
    There are more trees to save

THE PAST IS PROLOGUE

They say you can't go back again
        You can
but
        You can't

Return to those memories
        Nostalgic reminiscences
                Wallowing in sorrow
                        Bouncing in joy

Vague recollections of
        Past moments
                Then suddenly knowing
                        Why you fled

Racing from the smothering air
        The icy chill of fear
                Moments of ridicule
                        Bouts of loneliness

Visions of truth
        Dredged from the locked doors
                Of the unconscious mind
                        Suddenly wincing in the glare

Of the light of day
        Revealing the hidden memoirs
                Lurking in the cave of reality
                        Draped in the veil of fantasy

They say you can't go back again

You can

but

You can't.

A POET PONDERING I

A poet pondering her voice
Considering a range of choice
Finds either freedom or a curse
Will it be rhythm or free verse?

A POET PONDERING II

A poet pondering words as metaphors
          and images
Considers a myriad of poetic styles
          numbering in hundreds
Across this mindful chaos
          flies the elusive butterfly
 of voice and choice
          rhythm or free verse.

RECIPE FOR A WRITER'S LAMENT

A cup of ability
An ounce of flexibility
A pinch of credibility
A teaspoon of humility
Occasional viability

Add believability
Mixed with some tranquility
A dash of irritability
A smidge of vulnerability
Occasional fertility

Sweets for potability
Perhaps some instability
Then claim no liability
And no responsibility
Occasional sterility

Mix this impossibility
To thick attainability
And bake to suitability
Guaranteed reliability
Occasional reality

Take accountability
For its marketability
To publish with facility
Then wait until senility
Occasional achievability

SIGNING AT THE BOOK STORE

A spring-scented breeze wafting floral essence
Slips and slides around the door set ajar
Inviting readers to browse the shelves
Perhaps to purchase another book

Seated at the entrance, books displayed
An indy writer invites the breeze to
Gently cool her flaming cheeks
Painfully frozen in a welcoming smile

Belying an internal roiling in her gut
Sending a tsunami of anxiety in waves of
Blood rushing through a pulsing heart
Brain frantically seeking words to entice them

They nod and smile, then turn away quickly
Feigned interest in anything at hand but her
Seeking authors already bloated
With success and fame and fortune

In silence she bemoans her fate
Hidden behind a pretense of confidence
Another book signing from hell
Blowing away in the fragrant gentle breeze.

Florida State Poets Association Poetry Contest 2011
Second Honorable Mention

NATURAL PROGRESSION

Friends are like snowflakes.
Each a unique beauty,
blanketing us with love
and subtle alterations.

Swept away by the north wind
deserting us, shivering and alone,
until the next blizzard
and new friends drift in.

Memories linger
like the imprints on a window
of impaled snowflakes,
sparkling in the sunlight.

THE RUNAWAY

She fled her mistakes
To start again
She would change
And do it differently
This time

This time came
She mirrored her errors
Opportunity fleeing like smoke
Drifting to a new destination
Once again

Once again she failed the test
This time her own judge and jury
Sentenced to live in isolation
In circumstances beyond control
Facing truths

Facing truths of her own faults
Responsible for a life not lived
Now she understands
And weeps for wasted years
Lost chances

BLAME MOM

They said when they were young
It was the cat
Maybe the dog
Not me

Could be the goldfish
Not the turtle
Too slow
Not me

They said when they were 'tweens
It was the other kid
He did it
Not me

They shrugged when they were teens
They texted
Rolled their eyes
Mumbled
Not me

Blame Game when they grew up
It was Mom
She didn't do this, or did that
When they were young
Not their fault

LIES ABOUT MYSELF

Here I stand upon a daisy dotted hill
Blonde hair blowing in the wind
Whipping across blue eyes
Blinding them to nature's gifts

Tall and slender as the Aspen
Quivering against the gusts
Strong legs keeping balance
And a spine in perfect alignment

But I in arrogant youthful ignorance
Believe that life will always be such
I am the body electric
Glowing forever in the fullness of life

Until the maddening tick tick tick
Moves time inexorably forward
Into the realm of reality
And reflections ripple into truth

LIFE'S GIFT

Life's gift to us is change
       A chance to rearrange
              Ignore the prearranged
                     And make a fair exchange

Perhaps an alteration
       Or a tiny variation
              Some miniscule mutation
                     Thus breaking our stagnation

Compelling us to move
       Into a different groove
              Where we have to prove
                     What others disapprove

Although it may seem strange
       And sometimes disarrange
              Friendships that estrange
                     But…living equals change

GRATITUDE

When foulest forces may collude,
be strong is not a platitude
when offered up with attitude
of gratitude.

Even words that border crude
or vocal tones that echo rude
can belie the meaning hued
in gratitude.

Loving words that are construed
with overtones of hate imbued,
will bring a bounty much renewed
by gratitude.

Although an evil may allude
to messages that might delude,
seek and find the magnitude
of gratitude.

Should the negativity intrude,
never, ever just preclude
that all is lost, then sit and brood,
think gratitude.

When facing moral turpitude
and your self-esteem is skewed,
give yourself some latitude
of gratitude.

If circumstances foul include

no way to offer rectitude,
think in terms of fortitude
and gratitude.
Others may at times allude
to a negativity of mood,
then meditate in solitude
on gratitude.

Bygone days of servitude
lead to days of lassitude
resulting in a multitude
of gratitude.

If the jealous multitude
condemn you as a lazy dude,
shrug with happy certitude
and gratitude.

Be aware as you extrude
the facets of your pulchritude,
remember always to exude
your gratitude.

LIES WITHIN LIES

Why are there so many lies
Let loose to assault our lives
Perpetrated by liars
Convinced they know what's best

Liars who control and promote
Agendas that in the end
Become lies in themselves
When the truth emerges, too late

Like non-existent, invisible WMDs
or yellow, orange and red flags
Interchangeable after a while
And ignored like the boy who cried wolf

Behind the scenes machinations
Deals within deals
Back watching, back stabbing
Secret agreements to add this and that

Who cares about THEM
The folks outside the marbled halls
Far from the whispered voices
Of deal makers and king makers

Send them off to die
In some dot on the map
To reinforce more lies
That we are the saviors of the world

A word here, a rumor there

Hinting some horrific this or that
No substance, just innuendo
Enough to disturb the status quo

Friends who lie down with enemies
with their own selfish agendas
Hidden by fabrications and excuses
Seemingly unmoved by consequences

The cheaters and con-men
Fleecing the rich and the poor
Enlarging their girth with money belts
Bulging with green, the color of muck

The lies of family and friends
Who live in hedonistic glee
To mine own end be true
The hell with you or you or you.

Yesterday's liars wove the threads of time
Into tapestries of death and misery
Tapestries rotting in wooden coffins
Locked away by the liars of today

WE THE PEOPLE

What instills a surge of pride
In flags that waver hot and cold
When rockets fly and swords collide
And hunger grips the young and old

It's hard to muster loyalty
To leaders blind to peace and calm
They laud the beasts as royalty
And kneel before their mighty bomb

Oil and coal keep fires burning
Rich men profit from the poor
And young ones lose their homes and earning
The future hidden and obscure

Where is the patriot we praised
The drum beats and the marching bands
Sinking as the seas are raised
By global warming on the lands

Who will call a stop to greed
Who will end this march to death
Who will plant the precious seed
That saves life's last eternal breath

We the people!

THE WARRIOR'S GHOST

Holes where bullets pierced the fabric of the faded
uniform
Opening his life's blood to dry where medals might have
been
      Where gentle hands might have rested

He prowls the night, searching, ever searching for life lost
Eternally wondering why he cannot find it
      In this world between worlds

He wanders in lonely isolation amid the ravaged
battlefield
But cannot rest his weary body until he understands, but
never will
      Mama, where are you?

Seeking love he only dreamed of, children never to be
born
The life he might have had, had he…. What?
      The thought eludes his ragged mind

And so the warrior wanders, forever lost in his dreams
Never to be realized in this existence between worlds
      In this ghostly realm of death.

I was in my high chair according to my mother
When his lofty voice echoed from the radio
'This is a day that will live in infamy'
I opened my mouth for more, but her hand had frozen

Every day I waited for daddy to come home
dirty and sweaty from the Brooklyn Navy Yard.
I talked to him while he washed the grime from his
hands.
I don't remember if he ever answered me.

Around the corner they built tall buildings,
Nurses in starched white dresses and caps lived there
with WACS and WAVES in crisp uniforms,
while soldiers washed up on the shores of France.

We shopped at the A&P in Seagate.
Mommy had a book of stamps she used to pay for things.
She bought war bonds sold by a funny man with a pointy
beard
Wearing a red, white and blue suit and a tall black hat

Cousin Louis got shot on an island in the Pacific
He learned to carve peach pits and made monkeys for me
He was never the same Cousin Louis after that
He got very fat and died too young, leaving his wife and
son.

In seventh grade I cried when Daniel dumped me for
Marian.
Mothers cried when North Korea invaded South Korea

and the United States of America became the world's savior,
fighting the red menace of communism, whatever that was.

The war continued and I graduated to crinolines and poodle skirts.
Frankie and Judy gave way to Chubby and Elvis.
Bobby socks and saddle shoes segued into pumps and stockings.
We did the lindy, I loved Brando, and the police action ended.

In college, I met my love and knew it was serious.
His best friend came back from post-war Korea.
An MP in Seoul, he saw things no nice boy from Brooklyn
should ever see, and he wasn't ever the same.

My love joined the army reserve to keep from being drafted.
Then Russia planted missiles in Cuba, or said they did.
Seven months pregnant I waited as they read off the list of reserve units
to be deployed in case. His wasn't on the list.

Ever the guardian of world peace we entered Vietnam as observers,
giving a new meaning to the word, not in the dictionary.
For thirteen years I was a suburban wife, mother and closet hippy,
with long hair, poncho and guitar, singing of peace with Joan and Bob.

They died every day in a steamy jungle, a generation lost forever.

The survivors returned in ignominy to an angry America.

No ticker tape parades for these beaten, heroic warriors.

No statues, medals and rewards, just nightmares and PTSS.

What the hell was Grenada, where the hell was Grenada?

How did you even pronounce the damn place, long a, short a?

Another legacy so a second-rate actor could claim warrior status.

More mothers cried and the tide surged upon the beach.

At least I knew where Panama was located because of the canal.

A vague notion that drugs were involved, did anybody even care?

Another generation washed up on the shore to feed someone's ego

and right a wrong that could never be mended with dead bodies.

Then we moved to the hot deserts of the Middle East.

Again, America the Savior looms large to free some dot on the map,

leaving burning oil wells, the job unfinished and bodies in the sand,

opening the door to an invasion upon our soil and bodies falling from on high.

Another ego rides once more into the fray perilously seated

upon a steed worthy of a horseman of the apocalypse

The horseman detours a few hundred miles in a different direction
and the perpetrators escape while another generation is buried in the sand.

Now, in an attempt to re-adjust the compass point another ego rides
across the sands of time to fight an un-winnable war in a harsh land.
Another generation of men and women culled and damaged, families torn
and still the tide ebbs and flows with the pull of the moon.

After seventy years of war
we have lost our sanity
And too many generations
In a futile search for peace.

THE MYSTERY OF HISTORY

There exists a mystery
Descending through the ages
Lessons taught by history
Hide in musty pages

Crumbled, yellowed, long in tooth
Locked in darkened cages
Lurks the legacy of truth
Penned by learned sages

Lust for power, wealth and fame
Since the darkest ages
Supersedes the wisest claim
Peace not war engages

So we write this mystery
On the world's front pages
Lessons learned from history
Unlock golden ages

UNFINISHED LIVES

Not an auspicious day
An ordinary winter Friday
A week before the ending
Or the new beginning of the world

Only two days after 12-12-12
A day of ascendance and movement
When meteors raced across the sky
And planets began their prophetic alignment

On this ordinary December day
The world shook in fear and rage
As twenty tiny stars winked out
And darkness fell on unrealized dreams

When hope crashed in a hail of bullets
Unspun dreidels, unopened Chanukah gifts
Hidden Christmas toys waiting in vain
A red bike buried in a box never to be ridden

The unbearable agony of drifting souls
Reaching out for Mommy's arms
Their unfinished lives
Now only a fantasy

AGING HIPPY

I am the voice of the aging hippie
The singer of songs of freedom and love
The marcher protesting senseless wars
The burner of bras and draft cards

I am Lucy in the sky with diamonds
The dove sleeping in the sand
Still wondering where the flowers have gone
These forty years long passing

I still drive a golden bus in my dreams
The silver VW gleaming on her face
Sporting bumper stickers of peace
Plaid curtains flapping in the wind

I am the wearer of tie-dye tees
Wrapped in a poncho
A headband of flowers in my hair
Peace symbol upon my breast

I am the plucker of guitar strings
The suburban wife and mother
An actor on a stage
Creating the next generation

In my head are the memories
Beating the drums of change
Still marching to the fifes of war
Ringing the bells of freedom

Oh, when will they ever learn

ODE TO VINCENT

A dew-drop tear dangles
suspended in slow-motion time
from the tip of a petal
dipped in molten gold

A black Cyclops eye watches
the tear descend
stretching on a watery link
glinting in the sun's rising rays

By tomorrow's dawn
one golden petal will begin to fade
curling inward
the first to fall in the natural cycle

The evolving eye will watch
the daily drip of tears
until the end
when birds will feed on its seeds

Thank you Vincent
for immortalizing the golden petals
and engaging ebony eye

BE NOW

Let go the past
For it is gone
And cannot be redone

The future has yet to exist
An unknown entity
A glint in time

Live in this moment
Be now, be here
For in a wink it becomes the past

THE NATURAL WORLD

Meandering along the winding ways between middle years and elder years our senses savor a myriad of sights, sounds and smells. Now we comprehend the meaning of life around us and possess the language to express our feelings. Come join this traveler and experience a journey in the natural world that made her pause in awe, laughter and sadness. Imagine the natural world as a masterpiece of art, or the sound of musical notes, or a movie of nature in the raw.

We live in a three-dimensional theater that presents beauty at every turn, if we but stop and observe. These are moments that allow our whole being to rest from the bombardment of negativity that rains upon us every day. Come along and open your senses.

THE SCENTS OF NATURE

Blown in on the breeze
The clean sweet smell
Of early morning rain
Sparkling on new mown grass

Wafted in on the wind
The salty scent of the sea
And faint fragrances of fish
Mingle with hot wet sand

Stormy gusts in the squall
The odor of fear fueled by
The aroma of electric air
With each shaft of lightening

Blasting in on a blizzard
Icy fingers of frost
Freeze olfactory membranes
Memories of piney smoke

THE BLIGHT

Our Earth,
Raped ruins of lost
Forests, mountains, valleys
Plundered spoils destroying beauty,
She weeps.

Red tears,
Hot lava spews
Sliding down wizened cheeks,
Spreading a blanket on her breast;
She sleeps.

More pain,
Rivers cresting
Cooling muddy waters
Caress away the agony;
She sighs.

Tranquil
Long winter's sleep,
She wakens to warm sun.
A shy green shoot pushes upward;
She lives.

#17 Nevada Poetry Society Award

SUMMER SOUNDS

Old memories
Invading the brain
On hot summer nights

Crickets in the grass
Car horns blaring
Hot summer sounds

Country music
City music
Through the open window

SOUTHERN SUNSET

Blazing streaks of fire
A horizontal rainbow
Backdrop for the silhouette
Of tall twin palm trees
Nodding to the sinking sun

[Tanka]

LIFE IN REVERSE

Feathers sparkling in the sunlight
Like new snow upon the ground
The Ibis waits in weightless anticipation
Perched atop a quivering bush

Where lizards lurk, shivering
Under tiny green leaves
In ingrained fearful anticipation
Of imminent, torturous doom

In a blink and wink
The Ibis plunges a golden curved beak
Between the twigs and leaves
And plucks out a struggling lizard

That had just flicked its tongue
Scooping up a flitting mosquito
Filled with the succulent red liquid
Of the human it had just bitten

A pair of pop-eyes rise to the surface of the lake
Searching the shores for a busy bird
Catching succulent lizards for dinner
Such is life and death on Mirror Lake

Watery Perception
We perceive that water is clear
When removed from its source
Its elements invisible to the eye
A transparent living fundamental

Yet we perceive a blue sea
Trees reflected in a tranquil lake
Cottony clouds drifting above and below
Identical twins in a mirror image

Perhaps the lake sees mirages in
The world outside its realm
Borrowing for a brief time
Color and light for its own pleasure

A PALM'S EYE VIEW

Streaks of fire and ice
Rainbow backdrop for
Twin palm trees
Nodding to the rising sun

Tall palms dripping
Golden tinsel fronds
Waving to the tangerine rays
Of the sinking sun

A SNAPSHOT OF FLORIDA

Dancing diamonds sparkle on Mirror Lake
Flitting across the slate-gray surface
Rippling in the late afternoon sun
As the waving shadows of the trees lengthen

Watched closely by two territorial wood storks
A dainty Great White Egret wades along the shoreline
Snacking as he trolls for tasty tidbits before
Roosting somewhere secret for the night

The world turns and the sun drops to the horizon
Painting the sky in blazing red-orange flames
Sending fiery streaks of color across the water
Where tiny wavelets churn in the wind

The last vestiges of sunset, a dark orange backdrop
For the black silhouettes of twin undulating palm trees
The lake bathed in shades of silver, steel and pewter
A camera's view of a late Florida afternoon

A VIEW OF THE NATURAL WORLD

What I love about autumn are kaleidoscope colors
What I hate about autumn is the portent of passing
What I love about autumn is the crispy crunch of leaves
What I hate about autumn are the wheezy sneezes

What I love about winter are giant snowflakes
What I hate about winter is shoveling snow
What I love about winter are tinseled oak trees
What I hate about winter is slip sliding away

What I love about spring is the hatching hope
What I hate about spring is muddy in my mind
What I love about spring is emergence
What I hate about spring is pre-emergence

What I love about summer is cotton tee shirts
What I hate about summer is sweat
What I love about summer is the green
What I hate about summer is keeping the green

What I love about a sunrise is its flaming fires
What I hate about the sunrise is its portent for living.
What I love about a sunset is its fiery flame-out
What I hate about the sunset is the inevitable darkness

HAIKU

Crispy crunchy leaves
Kaleidoscope of colors
Wheezes and sneezes

WINTER'S SLEEP

Pale snow mounds lay upon the hill.
Icy fingers frost the glass
on windows holding back the blast
of cold that lurks upon the sill.

Clouds hang down heavy, dark and gray
frustrated by a pulsing urge
to spill forth fluids in a surge
of snow and sleet this dismal day.

Blackened tendrils wind and choke
a sleeping giant once in leaves
of verdant splendor robed, aggrieves
her nakedness and icy cloak.

Lie dormant now as silence sings.
Awaken us, oh warming sun.
Away the winter, life must come
from warming breath that springtime brings.

ENCOUNTERING A SYMPHONY ON A FRENCH MOUNTAIN AIR BY VINCENT D'INDIF, 1886

Calm
Flowing stream dappled by leafy light
Gentle creatures tiptoeing through forest glades

I sway, eyes closed.
Tempo rises
Faster, faster, cymbals crash.
Brass sing out
Fingers scoot up the piano from bottom to top
The French horn honors the earth.
All play in harmony
Earth is harmony
Flora and fauna, side by side
Beneath a dappled roof of sun and leaves

I am transported to dark mountain forests.

Smell of earthy loam
Decaying leaves
Fresh water

Sounds of birds twittering
Water spilling across rocks
Crackling twigs

Visions of green and brown
Sun speckled leaves
A white tail bunny
A spotted fawn
Feel of rough bark

Damp leaves
Light breeze
Cold water rushing through my fingers

I am a woodland fairy
Under a toadstool
Drinking dew from dripping leaves
Vivace, the music swells, staccato.
I fly across the damp rocks and rushing water
Over the flowing stream dappled by leafy light
Translucent wings beating the rhythm of the horn.

FLORIDA SUMMERS

Sticky, wet, hot and himid
Thunderstorms blasting the sky daily
Darkening the world to gray-black
Sending shards of lightning to earth

Torrents of rain pour from the clouds
In short bursts of life-giving liquid
To the joyous thirsty plants below
Roots rising up to the deluge

Crepe myrtle blossom
In shades of pink and fuscia
Rising above hibiscus unfolding
Giant blooms of blazing fire

The lake flows in tranquil peace
Blue herons feeding along it's shores
Watching pelicans dive-bomb for fish
Black anahingas spreading their wings to dry

Stately storks and cranes parade
A ballet dance of precision and grace
Brown ducks and white cattle egrets
Skirt the alligator sunning on the grass

This is Florida in summer
A melange of sun and storm
White clouds and black
Still water and roiling surf

HAIKU

Droplets of damp dew
Trickles of weeping cloud tears
Shining leaves glisten

HAIKU

Sun sparkled dew drops
Crackling fall leaves underfoot
Rain-scented breezes

HARBINGERS OF SPRING

They descended into the yard today
Small feathered harbingers of spring
Red breasts reflecting the sun's rays
Brown feathers settling on downy backs

They covered the grass of surrounding yards
Roofs writhed with living, breathing shingles
There were hundreds, too many to count
For they did not stand still long enough

They mingled and pecked at invisible food
Hidden in browned winter grass
Others looked on from high perches
On both sides of the brackish still lake

They came in February for a brief picnic
Then left, a black mass against the setting sun
On the long, slow, northward journey home
Leaving behind the promise of spring

HUNGRY SNAKE

Slithering along the muddy bank
Half immersed in murky water
Hungry snake flicks his forked tongue
In anticipation of a repast

Seeking the blissfully unaware
A slimy toad or sunning lizard
To sting into immobility
And slake snake's gnawing hunger

HOT SUMMER NIGHTS, THE BRONX, NY, LATE 1940'S

      I simmer in my bed,
sweat bubbling.
Flowered curtains frame a rhinestone dipper
scooping liquid air.
      Moonlight plays tag on shadowy walls,
where ghostly figures dance.

Tangled in twisted, slimy sheets,
I suck the hot, sticky air,
Seeking a tiny waft of breeze
      to part the thickness.

The cacophony of the city assaults my ears.
Footsteps clack on baking asphalt.
Cars blare and honk like wild animals.
Sharp sirens wail and howl
      in concert with feral cats.

Imagine crisp icy snow.
Licking a popsicle.
Dangling feet in a cold lake
Opening the refrigerator.

Angry fists punch the pillow,
      then collapse.
Too hot.
More sweat.

Imagine a green forest
an icy stream

a star in the coldness of space.
      I close my eyes.

A breeze floats across my face.
Light replaces shadow.
The moon is the sun
      Night is erased.

OCTOBER GOLD

Rainbow colors of autumn hues
in vibrant shades of golden reds,
mask the crisply drying, dying leaves
struggling to stay aloft,
as they spiral slowly to the earth.

Death hidden in its flames
waving in the icy wind
as if to ward off the looming cold.
Begging one more day of Indian Summer
and the warm caress of the sun.

Naked empty trees
await a wintry coat of ice.
Roots of life snugly nesting
beneath the crunchy brown coat
that they once proudly, greenly wore.

And I delight and yet despair
as motley tints of orange and black
herald another Halloween
coming faster every year
as my life surges on.

Born on the night of witches, goblins, and ghosts,
spooky spirits roaming through the darkness,
tripping over grinning pumpkin faces.
A new baby wailed and another life began at
the final hour of October Gold.

OPENING WINTER'S FROSTY EYES

Opening winter's frosty eyes
Blinking at a sun-filled morn
Awakening to sleepy sighs
Light pushes at the dawn

Blinking at a sun-filled morn
Birds unfold their feathered wings
Light pushes at the dawn
They stretch their throats and sing

Birds unfold their feathered wings
To greet the warm sun's rays
They stretch their throats and sing
A joyous hello to the day

To greet the warm sun's rays
Tiny buds erupt to flowers
A joyous hello to the day
In green and verdant bower

Tiny buds erupt to flowers
A nod to burgeoning spring
In green and verdant bower
A wren unfurls its wings

A nod to burgeoning spring
Awakening to sleepy sighs
A wren unfurls its wings,
Opening winter's frosty eyes.

Fran Orenstein
58

THE COLOR OF RAIN IN FLORIDA

Green grass,
sparkling in sunlight.
Crimson hibiscus,
electric in the saturated air.

Blue plumbago,
dripping flowers.
Creamy magnolias,
against dark green leaves.

White gardenias,
petals gleaming.
Fuchsa crape myrtle,
waving at the clouds.

Rain, the harbinger of color,
Thunder, the drumming of the gods,
Lightning, the beautiful, dangerous siren.
Calling forth the onset of summer.

SEVEN A.M. IN SOUTH CAROLINA

Dawn, a fiery backdrop for silhouetted trees
Black sticks in January's cold winter
Sleeping giants awaiting warmth
To waken and stretch.

Painting word pictures of a new morning
No paints, pastels, pencils.
Mundane words describing flaming streaks
Reducing them to sighted memory.

Hot rainbow stripes in layers
Yellow, gold, orange, red,
Deep purple clouds tinged with pink
Floating in an emerging pale blue sky.

Can ears imagine what eyes can see?
Can words replace pictures?
Ask a sightless person in a world of darkness.
Ask a soundless person in a world of silence.

Seven a.m. in South Carolina
The stark, dark profile of the Preserve
A lone Magnolia in the foreground,
Blackened green against the blazing dawn.

SEVEN P.M. IN ARIZONA

The red-orange ball drops behind the peaks
Of the White Tank Mountains,
Spreading fiery tinged stripes
across the robin's egg blue sky.

Puffs and streaks of rare white clouds turn coral,
Absorbing the flames of the descending sun as
Saguaros lift their arms in a final moment of warmth
Before the desert cools.

There is no twilight here;
Only a blazing sunset,
Suddenly descending into night,
Obliterating all color and warmth.

STORM LUMINOSITY

An eerie glow invades the air
Between land and water
And the firmament of space
A darkness, yet not dark

Heavy bands of thunderous clouds
A gray-black overhang, hover
Blocking the ice blue sky
And puffy cotton-ball formations

Suspended like a glowering roof
Sent to cover the world
In eerily translucent luminosity
A darkly rich, terrifying beauty

A landscape changed in sharp relief
Reds and pinks of flowers glow
Against the darkening sky
Greens heightened in the darkling light

Great rolls of thunder fiercely echo
Like giant monster finger snaps
Lanced by shards of lightening bolts
Piercing the eerie storm-light

SUMMER IN THE SPRING

The news shows videos of happy families
Flocking to beaches along Florida's Gulf coast
Children build elaborate sand castles
Hunting for pink shells in the white sand

Parents sun on colorful beach chairs
Keeping a careful eye on their children
Who test the wavelets with their tiny toes
Screaming at the water lapping at their legs

Surfers ride the gentle waves awaiting the big one
Boats drift, silhouetted against the horizon
Screeching white seagulls hungrily search for scraps
Along the pristine western shoreline that edges Florida

The announcer comments on the early turnout
People cannot wait for summer to arrive officially
For in the distance a black mass oozes landward
Like a sci-fi creature smothering all in its wake

Come summer, the white sugar sand may be black
With tar balls, dead birds and bloated beached mammals
By July, the humans get in their oil-dependent cars
Turning their backs on the disaster of 2010

WATER LILIES

Those desiring a pristine lake
Call these interlopers weeds
They cry for extermination
But the water lilies fight back

Growing and multiplying
They invade the environment
Spreading their green plates
Further along the shoreline

Then one day a reddish cup of leaves
Spreads apart pushing forth
A spiky white flower with long petals
And a fuzzy yellow center peeking out

In a time when frogs abounded
They sat upon the lily pads
Puffing tiny chests and croaking
Flicking tongues at passing flies

Today the frogs are gone
Tomorrow the lilies will follow
And the lake will be pristine again
Until it too disappears into history

WEATHER PERSONIFIED

Dog Days of Summer

Smothering wet heat
Cloying air stifling the breath
Sapping energy

Old Man Winter

Wearing a white shroud
He flies in on the north wind
Breathing icy frost

Indian Summer

Fall leaves turning gold
Hints of icy winter's freeze
Hot days reappear

[Golden Trillium]

HAIKU

Falling stars erupt
In waves of sparkled colors
A big booming blast

FOURTH OF JULY

Flags lined walkways
Myriad stripes and stars waving
At all who passed by
Publicizing patriotism

Flags flew from tall poles
Telling the world
These people are true patriots
Unabashed in their advertising

I hung the flag in the window
A personal gesture to the holiday
A small flag no one saw behind the trees
But me, proud of what I believe

THE ELDER YEARS

As time moves inexorably on, the aging body
continues on its trek along the shifting sands.
Not knowing when the road will end, the elder
plods along, understanding the future now looms
finite, and far reaching plans are not to be.
Life reveals a shorter menu of choices, before
infirmity sets in or inevitable death intervenes.
The elder swallows the lumps of panic and fear in
the darkness of the night.
When the sun rises and the elder awakens, that is
another day of life to rejoice and say thank you.

THE FORWARD MARCH

Events that mark the passages of life
Seen through aging eyes
Blurring cataract vision
Tiny wrinkles fanning at the edges

Down the winding path
That narrows as the years pass
Diminishing physical ability
Clouding mental acuity

Retrospectives
Memoirs
Photographs
Fading dreams

Yet we march forward
Ever hopeful of something
Around the next curve
Over the next rise

WHAT IF...

They say what is done, cannot be undone
The past if altered, alters future lives
What if that were true, and all todays were not tomorrows
Would you still step into the fold of space

To venture back and erase the deeds of yesterday
Say no instead of yes, choose a different path
What if it were true you might not exist today
For time was changed by your reemergence as you

Different lovers, generations never born
Another life perhaps shorter but more exciting
What if you had the knowledge of today
Creating a profound effect upon tomorrow

The past beckons through the wrinkle in time
A siren's call to greatness, bringer of peace
What if it were you, that singular soul of change
If not for a simple decision made once upon a time

THE INEVITABLE DAY

Each year there is a special day
A mosaic, montage overlay
No pleas are heard that can delay
The forward march of our decay

Looked upon another way
That fateful, dreaded, dreary day
Can open gates to an array
Of treats upon life's silver tray

So if we cannot back away
From that inevitable day
Unless we fade and pass away
Let's sing…Happy Birthday!

LIES ABOUT MYSELF

Here I stand upon a daisy dotted hill
Blonde hair blowing in the wind
Whipping across blue eyes
Blinding them to nature's gifts

Tall and slender as the Aspen
Quivering against the gusts
Strong legs keeping balance
And a spine in perfect alignment

But I in arrogant youthful ignorance
Believe that life will always be such
I am the body electric
Glowing forever in the fullness of life

Until the maddening tick tick tick
Moves time inexorably forward
Into the realm of reality
And reflections ripple into truth

ENDINGS AND BEGINNINGS

Life's path meanders in a straight line
With joyous stops along the way
Creating memories to cherish

Then, it sharply turns and hugs the cliff
And we must cling to the edge
Or fall into the abyss of despair

Those memories along the way
Allow us to clutch the rocks with fingers
Stiffened by fear and grief

Knowing that in the unknown
New memories will form
And love will never fly away

WISDOM

Philosophically it is considered the age of wisdom
Chronologically referred to as the wisdom of age
Paradoxically simply an elusive illusion
Biologically altered gray matter of a hoary sage

For what remains of thoughts and musings
Fraught with enlightened experience
Lessons learned from deeds far gone
Rebellion interspersed with compliance

Do they heed the wisdom of the aged minds
Take unto themselves this precious knowledge
Freely given by the last generations of elders
Presented as an extraordinary privilege

Go away old man and let me live my life
They think in absolute despair
I can do it myself old woman
Go rock in your old rocking chair

THE MEMORY PARADE

Disparate memories parade
Across the ridges and valleys
Of a beleaguered brain
Like ants marching in rigid rows

Ancient memories claw at
Sheer walls of dark caverns
Seeking light and liberation
To torment another hapless soul

Memories set free by song or smell
A shadowy image in the corner of the eye
Recalled in a barrage of tears
Wistful smiles or a raucous laugh

Hidden deep in niches carved
Into the stone walls of the mind
They hide from enlightenment
That would blast apart the memory parade.

CREAKY KNEES

When creaky knees seize and lock
Or inflexible, arthritic hips groan
When swollen fingers refuse to grasp
Then what remains is but the moan

The memories of athlete's bursting
Through the finish line of the games
The honor of awards for prowess
Now diminished by the gnawing pains

Of aging joints and crooked backs
But deep within the recesses of the mind
Remain the glory days of nimble youth
Pain-free, agile exploits left behind

Consider those who do not reach this age
Who fall beside the twisting, bumpy road
Never to recall the days of youth
Whose pain will never be a heavy load

You have arrived to live in quiet days
Accomplishing deeds as yet unsung
Pursuing not the glory or the prize
But things you could not do when you were young.

MIND CONTROL

Hear me brain
I say again
There is no gain
In feeling pain

You work in vain
I tell you plain
You must abstain
From sending pain

Must I sustain
This old refrain
It's not humane
To send me pain

I will restrain
And then retrain
'Til you retain
There's no more pain

I can't complain
You're very sane
I love you brain
BUT NO MORE PAIN

AGED KNOWLEDGE

Great age closes the door to new ideas
and critical thinking

For many people, long past education
Or never educated

Don't think in learned terms
Or seek the learning now

The past is at the forefront of the conscious mind
Memory is a time capsule

The future is a known entity
and time eclipses.

MEMORIES

Caught in the cobwebbed corners of the mind
Musty memories struggle to revive
Amid the chaos of elapsed time
Pushing against an impermeable wall.

Surfacing to breathe
Gasping to retrieve
Some faint semblance
Of elusive remembrance

A forgotten face arising in the mind's eye
A name escaping into the ether
Fading in the fog shrouded mist
Just beyond the edges of reclamation

In the cacophony
Of disharmony
Slipping, sliding
Words eliding

Memory strains against the web of recall
Come back lost words, forgotten names
Haunting faces fading like sepia prints
Drifting ever further back into obscurity.

THE FATEFUL DAY

In one lifetime there may be many
Or perhaps too few
But still they come with regularity
Like ocean waves upon the shore

Erasing etchings in the sands of time
Wiping aside past deeds
Cleaning the slate to write anew
Creating a different time-line

Yet there is always one
The apocalypse of those days
Anticipated with fear and loathing
A heavy curtain obscuring the future

The one that dominates all others
Tolling as a death knell to life
Forcing the mind to face the reality
Of goals unmet and lives trampled

A curlicue gate bars the road
Opening to a fog-shrouded landscape
On that day, step through
And the metal gate slams and locks

Glimpsed through the scrollwork
The one-way road left behind
Curves and fades into nothingness
Terrible loss grips the heart

Terror of the unknown unravels the mind

Fran Orenstein
80

Visions of death's demons lurking in the fog
Where the cracked and murky path splits
Winding and turning in opposite directions
To isolate one day to bear the weight
Of a lifetime
Is denying the choice of paths
Into the possibilities we can still experience

HOLLOW HOLES

Emptiness
        A hollow hole
        Filled with air
                Looming nights
        Wasted time…moving fast.

Hunger
        A hollow hole
        Filled with chocolate
                Junk food
        Hot soup…burning palette

Anger
        A hollow hole
        Filled with gnawing gut monsters
                Clenched fists
        Stiff neck…headache

Pity
        A hollow hole
        Filled with tears
                Yearning dreams
        Fantasy worlds…unrealized

Despair
        A hollow hole
        Filled with nothing
                Until hope
        Falls into the abyss…gone

THE LONE ONE

Adrift in a mass of humanity
the lone one roams through life
yearning to belong
to be an insider
one of the mindless multitude

It hovers at the edge
tentative, hopeful
outside crowded rooms
peering in, seeing no place,
no beckoning hand

Staring through barred windows,
knocking on locked doors,
waiting to be welcomed,
seeking inclusion in…whatever.
bereft in solitude, it drifts on.

Wandering desolate, on teeming roads
alongside the hoards,
never within their realm,
driven to tears by invisibility
by exclusion

Unseen, the lost one walks
beside the crowd,
losing the game of musical chairs
with no seat in the circle of life.
always standing beside, outside

The lost one bears witness to life

excluded from inclusion
screaming voice unheard
muted words diluted to silence
in the babble of human discourse

BREAST CANCER REVISITED

A quarter of a century passes
A single cell in isolation
Starving for life returns in
Bones and nodes

Awakening in a nanosecond
Swelling and growing
Reproducing and invading
Bones and nodes

There is no why, no why me
Another flicker in the timeline of life
You don't feel the misery in
Bones and nodes

A MISSIVE TO THE PURVEYOR OF DEATH

Have you returned yet again
Haunting with dispassionate cruelty
To mar and maim without a care
Ravaging mind and body
Mindless destructor

Where lies your lust for raining
Sheets of pain upon the soul
Rendering the heart to slivers
Of dreams once more denied
And crushed

Once thwarted by the strength
Of mortal fortitude and knowledge
You take another plunge
Determined at all cost to win
This time

Faced with new avenging armies
Cursed by every living cell
A pariah of invading destruction
You melt before the magic sword
Of defeat

Slithering into a slimy mire
To be sucked away for all eternity
Into to the sewers of hell
To burn in a fiery furnace
Ever more

Tranquility and peace transcend

Fran Orenstein

The blackness of your deeds
You cannot rise against

SILENT WORLD

Silence…
No one called today.
No one rang the bell.
Mail silently delivered.

Nothing broken.
No repairman broke the stillness.
The gardener did not appear.
Only the ducks quacked.

The cat,
a quiet companion
of incomprehensible language
pet me…feed me.

Is this all there is
at the end of days,
an Eleanor Rigby ending,
dying in silence?

In stillness
I wait for the day's end.
Sunset across the lake
flaming out in a silent rage of red.

Perhaps tomorrow
the phone will ring,
the doorbell will chime,
human connection.

THE FORGOTTEN MOTHER

What is a good mother
Who is she to be revered
In song and poem
Beloved by all

What is a bad mother
Who is she to be reviled
In song and poem
Abhored by all

Do not both scream
In agonizing pain
When pushing forth
The ungrateful child

Wincing at the pulling
On nipples tender and raw
Opening the engorged breast
To disgorge life-giving liquid

Is it not their lips that kiss
Their hands that stroke
Their arms that hold
Their words that soothe

Who stands in judgment
Of a mother's sacrifices
The sleepless nights spent
Listening to baby's raspy breath

Crying with their every tear

Aching with their every fall
Going without so they eat well
And wear the latest fashion

Finally, when her life is hers
It is too late to reclaim the years
Of youth and health
She lives alone, far away

For they have abandoned her
And moved on with lives
So full there is no space
For her, the giver of their lives

A GRANDMOTHER'S LAMENT

Who are these small strangers
Growing older, as am I
Unconnected to my life
Kept away in distant places.

> Would I know them
> If we met by chance
> Recognize their faces
> Take a second glance

Do they look at all like me,
Perhaps the curly hair
Or is it some ancestral gene
From the other side

> Would I know them
> Walking down the street
> Sense a connection
> There, but incomplete

What do they dream or desire
What flames their passions
Are they thinkers or doers
Leaders or followers

> Would I know them
> In a crowded room
> Feel their presence
> Descendants of my womb

All the years lost in separation

Will they one day say in tremulous tones
Where were you all this time, Granny
I thought you didn't love me any more
        Would I have an answer
        Something to explain
        The aching disconnection
        The never-ending pain

Though time lost will never be reclaimed
Constant and deep is my love for you
That crosses distance, time and space
And transcends life and death, forever

Fran Orenstein

THE LONELY SOUL

Beware the lonely soul
who walks among us,
touching but not touched,
loving but not loved.

The moist hand reaching out,
pulling back empty,
fearful of rejection,
yearning for connection.

The soul who lives in solitude,
wandering alone and sad
through the bare rooms of life,
unnoticed by the world.

Emptiness
Darkness
A void in the wilderness
A black hole in space

Tears edging toward the precipice,
preparing to leap
into the unknown,
to crash on the rocks below

The heart, an empty cavern
where love and passion might dwell.
The throat knotted, closed
to the sweet juices of living.

Yearning...but

Lost…
Lonely…and
Alone

ABANDONED MOTHER

She is left behind, bereft
    The abandoned mother
Adult children moving on
    Never looking back

How long will she wander
    Alone through life
Remembering the long labors
    The years of love

Sacrifice and devotion
    Forgotten mistakes
Forever remembered
    By those children

Her flaccid breasts weep
    Her shrunken womb aches
The seeds of generations
    Shriveled and lost

She fears the empty road
    That looms ahead
Winding through time
    Smooth, cobbled, cratered

Cane in hand she plods onward
    And dreams of laughing
Voices around the table
    Now set for only one

They rarely call or write

These children of her heart
Is she even a vague memory
This abandoned mother

THE VEIL OF LONELINESS

So many possibilities lost
Blunted by the unrelenting
    Veil of loneliness.

Love passing just out of reach
Despite the cries of the lonely voices
    To me, come to me

Friendship, fleeting and fickle
Changing on a word or a gesture
    Unenduring, elusive

Empty nights spent alone
Silent days without contact
    Talking to the air

Solitary decisions
No voice to argue
    No discussion, no dissension

Solitaire and computer games
Devoid of competition
    Jokes and laughter

The hostess looks behind you
How many?
    Table for one in the corner

The veil of loneliness falls
Blurring the experience
    Of small pleasures

The pain begins deep inside
Choking the throat
            Overflowing the eyes

Loneliness does that.

Florida State American Association of University Women,
poetry contest, 2008-2009.
Free verse second place

WE OWN OUR DESTINY

A salute to William Shakespeare

All the world's a stage…
And all the men and women write their roles
As befits their nature and their nurture
Evolving as human, or not

Entering stage right, a child
Innocent and pure
Gathering the flotsam and jetsam
Of life's offerings along the way

Exiting stage left, an elder
Knowing and wise
Leaving in his or her wake
A memorable life…or not.

THE ESTATE SALE

Death, the indiscriminate procurer of souls
Claims the next traveler on the road to infinity
A stubborn, frightened, wary old woman
Not yet ready to leave this sordid world

Instead, she hovers, bathed in misty invisibility
Staring in bewildered, bleak humiliation
At her world, scattered on tables in the grimy garage
Tossed like so much trash by uncaring hands

Her naked life displayed for all to see
Bearing witness to the world of her existence
Things she kept hidden behind closed doors
Private things she coveted and loved

Blue-flowered china cups and chipped dishes
Unmatched silverware and glasses
Her collection of glass paper weights
The ceramic cats she carefully cleaned

There, a half-squeezed tube of toothpaste
Here, a shell-shaped soap dish and faded towels
Her precious linens once folded and stacked
Now lying helter-skelter on musty tables

She sees strangers fingering her tea towels
Arguing over the value of her wedding silver
Sitting in her worn recliner, her private retreat
Pawing through her clothing, laughing at her taste

If spirits could weep, she would flood the world

Fran Orenstein
100

With tears of shame at this invasion of her life
Now reduced to displays on card tables and
A box of panty-liners shouting her incontinence

Beaten down, she turns toward the beckoning light
Leaving the last remnants of a life she no longer lived
And a once beautiful home she no longer inhabited
Now existing in a dimension where she no longer
belonged.

A FOOLS REFRAIN

In skin that burns with heat of shame
I wish to play the act again
Recall the words I said in vain
And hope they all forget my name

Words we speak do not reframe
But lie in wait like lurking pain
Unwanted memories remain
To rise unbidden in the brain

In squirming agony we claim
The words and deeds that do defame
Our pride in what we may attain
Diminished by past deed's disdain

A GRANDMOTHER'S BIRTHDAY WISH

A missive flew into the firmament
drifting among the stars
A wish for a special gift
Lost grandchildren returned

Grinding pain and anguish
Years of tears and sorrow
The agony of not knowing them
An empty vessel unfilled

Today's he turned thirteen
This beautiful grandson I barely know
I sent a card and a ten dollar bill
Thinking it was just a token gift

For never had they acknowledged
Any gift, so this was compromise
Something small, a gesture
Just to say I'm still here thinking of you

At four o'clock the cell phone rang
A young man's voice no longer a child
He told me in the brief words
Of thirteens about his life

Then his sister, an almost sweet sixteen
Filled in the blanks of her life
The dreams of college, boys she befriended
Girls she unfriended and her academics

We ended the call with a promise to keep in touch

I wept tears of joy and gratitude
That someone heard my message floating in the clouds
And sent the children of my child back to me

Fran Orenstein
104

ME AND MYSELF

I will just be me
Here in this moment
Alone in myself
A finite moment in time
Simply to be me

THE INEXORABLE TICK-TOCK

She went home
To be with family
The dream cut short

A new life dangling
On a fragile thread of numbers
"I'll be back," she promised
Her words taken on the breeze

Time moved on
Her clock wound down
Yet I wait for her return

A promise is a promise

A WOMAN OF A CERTAIN AGE

On this day of celebration
A woman of a certain age
Contemplates the paths she chose
And others she passed by

Where would her life have led
Had she but stepped upon the other road
The second choice, perhaps the third
A path less traveled on

Memories of people loved
Of happiness and friendship
Existing only as vague dreams
Had she turned the other way

The woman of a certain age
In wistful observation
Sees her footprints in the earth
Then nods and smiles

FINALE

So ends these episodes of a life
of seven decades.
There is more to come
for life continues...
until the final breath.

Thanks for reading my book. If you enjoyed it, please take a moment to leave me a review at your favorite online-retailer.

Connect with me on Social Sites

Twitter: https://twitter.com/Hubysmom
Facebook: https://www.facebook.com/fran.orenstein.1
LinkedIn: https://www.linkedin.com/pub/dr-fran-orenstein/1b/278/295
Website: http://www.franorenstein.com

Discover other titles by Fran Orenstein

Adult Novels
Danse Macabre
Death in D Minor
Murder in Duplicate
Gaia's Gift

Chapter Books
Amber and the Whipped-Cream Dress
One Amber Too Many

'Tween Books
Fat Girls From Outer Space
The Shadow Boy Mysteries, a Trilogy

Young Adult
The Book of Mysteries, a Single-Volume Series
The Calling of the Flute
The Spice Trader's Daughter

Poetry
Reflections (Out of Print)
Five Six Pick Up Sticks (Out of Print)

ABOUT THE AUTHOR

Fran Orenstein, Ed.D., is the award-winning author of novels, short stories, and poetry for kids, 'tweens, teens, and adults. She wrote her first poem at age eight and submitted a short story to a magazine at age twelve. Fran has been a teacher, written professionally as a magazine editor/writer, counseled people with disabilities, and also wrote political speeches, newsletters, legislation, and promotional material while working for New Jersey State Government for twenty-two years.

She has published academically, and written professional papers on gender equity and violence prevention, which she presented at national and international conferences. Fran managed programs for women in gender equity, childcare, and disabilities, as well as serving as Special Projects and Disabilities Officer for the AmeriCorps Commission in New Jersey.

Fran has a BA in Early Childhood Education, a MEd in Counseling Psychology, and an Ed.D. in Child and Youth Studies.

She especially loves writing for kids and teens, and considers her children and grandchildren her best inspiration.

All Fran's books are available at on-line bookstores in EBook and paperback form

www.ingramcontent.com/pod-product-compliance
Lightning Source LLC
Chambersburg PA
CBHW032010040426
42448CB00006B/564